FIELD GUIDE *A TEMPO*

FIELD GUIDE
A TEMPO

Henry Walters

The Hobblebush Granite State Poetry Series, Volume IX

HOBBLEBUSH BOOKS

Brookline, New Hampshire

Composed in Adobe Arno Pro at Hobblebush Books

Printed in the United States of America

ISBN: 978-1-939449-06-1

Library of Congress Control Number: 2014948951

Thanks to the journals where many of these poems first appeared: *Asymptote, Better Magazine, Broad Street, Echolocation, Kindred, The Literary Bohemian, Miracle Monocle, Persephone,* and *Tuesday: An Art Project.*

Cover art: Giotto di Bondone (1266–1336). Saint Francis preaching to the birds. Predella, oil on wood, 31.3 × 16.3 cm. INV309.
Photo: Daniel Arnaudet. Musée du Louvre
© RMN-Grand Palais / Art Resource, NY

G-Clef/Ampersand block prints by Henry Walters

The Hobblebush Granite State Poetry Series, Volume IX
Editors: Sidney Hall Jr. and Rodger Martin

HOBBLEBUSH BOOKS
17-A Old Milford Road
Brookline, New Hampshire 03033

www.hobblebush.com

to you long-gone nameless minstrels, gleemen, balladmongers,
who trebled your troubles for nothing & nobody at a crossroad

& to you ever-living Happy Hoosiers, singing your authorless
songs into a hard-of-hearing tape recorder & one another's ear

& to the threefold snow-angel with the stolen violin under her chin

Contents

Suppose I try to describe faithfully the prospect which a strain of music exhibits to me. The field of my life becomes a boundless plain, glorious to tread, with no death nor disappointment at the end of it. All meanness & trivialness disappear. I become adequate to any deed. No particulars survive this expansion; persons do not survive it. In the light of this strain there is no thou nor I. We are actually lifted above ourselves.

—THOREAU

~

Ourselves in the tune as if in space,
Yet nothing changed, except the place . . .

—STEVENS

~

This will prove a brave kingdom to me,
where I shall have my music for nothing.

—STEPHANO, *THE TEMPEST*

Da Capo

Reader, there's something I wish you could see, which you may not. It's very small, & its jar is large, like one waxwing in the loose weave of the sky. But I have no power to magnify. What I have to show I show you from afar, the field of view, in full: spruces shading out one side, a mill-stream changing pace along another, hoofprints in step with foxes following on the furthest edge. I can show you the lepidopterist with his long white net, the erratic leaps & lunges of his chase. The course he follows is a guessing game, the fugue of another, that of the thing he's after, a flying object, grace-note, winged erratum, unidentified, the score you are forbidden to see, & the seal upon his brow & upon this book.

Saw Instrumental

Rathlin Island

Across the handsaw drawn—as across the world
now seems—her fiddlebow—a whetting, whittling down
to two dimensions—a plane edge-toothed as ocean's own—
horizon-fretted—wind aslant a treeless (I would
have you listen to it) island—back/forth—(how, o
dare I, how to tell you?)—Ariel—(slit-bound)—
as once your forefinger set a wine glass humming—bone-
less, lungless sprite fast in the cloven pine-rings wailed

& bent his pitch (how high?) within that windbent tree—so
that night her saw—sighting, aligning, sliding between—
shrieked out (& never cross the grain) the Lilliputian
stars—made of the room, walls, floorboards, table, us, a mouth—
an echo chamber—until we heard our worldsend through
the crack-(my heart)(she played Amazing Grace)-less distance.

After Ariel

Assembling anything this delicate,
   dismantle
   your material
resources. As in, push back (lightly, lightly)
   the marble
   statue's cuticles
till crescent moons come rising up below.

As in, see the lunatic soaking Lear undo
   his buttons
   to make wind-openings.
As in, give fire holes for its alchemy.
   As in,
   our maple syruping
will take all day, boiling, bottling, giving away.

As in, mind how memorable magic is
   its own
   timely disappearance,
how, when you look to the clock in the theater,
   gone
   are its two slight hands.
As in, before us, suddenly birds of the air

take off, lightly, lightly, their marrowless
   fluted bones
   a feathered skeleton
cage that frees them. It *is* them, as a churchyard angel
   is stripped-down stone,
   a naked simpleton
flight of silent fancy, worn by the rain.

My ear's alembic wants a whoosh of flame
   to distill
   one miracle
from the rest: solstice-speck of a kestrel rising
   like sap in a maple,
   dawn-red decibel
with all its fingers hidden in the wings.

PRESTO

Let's play for real this time, I mean it, no matter what, the first one to speak is It, & after that it's the thing you say that's It, alright, but after that, it's the way you say whatever you say that's It, that's it, no matter what time it is, at school, or recess, if the teacher talks, it's how she talks that's It, & even at dinner, or taking a bath, or if you're asleep, let's say, if you talk in your sleep & I hear you & it's like you're talking to men on the moon, that's it, you're talking to men on the moon, alright, no matter what, if you're wearing clothes or not or if you're happy or sad or not, I mean it, or if you're talking like you're dead that's it you're dead, alright, or if you're dead for real, let's say, & it's like you're talking to me that's it you're talking to me, no matter what, & if tomorrow if I talk like you that's it I'm talking you, alright, I mean it, no matter what, for real this time.

Plumbing

The tap knows two felicities, the hot,
the cold, & all of it through the fingers,
unaccountable, like laughter. Which
of you, said king to courtiers,
could go a day & night foregoing sleep
& food & drink & draw
my lady's steaming bath the morning after
with silver sieve & spoon?

No dowser whittling at his witching cane.
No sleight-of-hand man with his patter & rhymes.
The natural fool, unschooled, for whom
the impossible's just one more playground game
of queens who shriek like songs when down
they dip one foot to the basin's brim.

Capture the Flag

If the poles of these two hemispheres
Are jails—ours the pump
That drew the Michigan iron-water up, & yours
The boxelder stump
High as a horseblock facing out to the road—
Forgive us, we knew no better.
Go play, say all the mothers,
Not where to draw the fairest boundaries
Nor how to make
The kitchen rag in plain sight not be seen,
Nor how to sneak
In noble fashion,
Nor how not to use deceit
To lure the others out of no-man's land
Onto your side
& haul them off, resisting, laughing,
Pleading innocence, to prison.
Freed & bound & freed
Again, grazing on edges, up to nothing,
The most unlikely plays the vigilante
Angel, righteous,
Her conscience criminal & unscathed.
Way off, at a distance furthered by the speed
Of the guards on watch
& your own slowfooted apprehension,
They beg to be saved—
Brothers, sisters, distant cousins,
Crying you mercy until the blood
Rises in you as to a rusty wellhead,
From roundabout reconnaissance on tiptoe
Spilling out

Into the sudden thoroughbred desire
To make a run, to race by where they stand
Chained to their block,
& give them a free ride back—
& in the sprint
Let your momentum pull you out of bounds
A little ways & further,
Where the long grass slows you to a wade
& bees in the hawkweed
Skirt you like showering Perseids,
& the wren in the brushpile natters but sits tight,
& the sandy ground
Like an endless hiding place
Keeps track of your prints for a day or so
But lets
You go again, unshod & riderless,
Swishing your tail & hunting much too
Hard, & fast,
For the single thing you'll never see,
Here, look,
In your most native & familiar spot,
Hidden, all along, right
Here, under your forelock,
Blue-black nest like a shadowy
Knothole in the night,
The whinnying thought.

Dramatis Personae

You, who play the parts
 Me, your understudy
  & One More, the wayward sphinxy lady who in a hunch & holey pointe shoes limps up Main in the morning & turns back down it at midday & evenings stands stock still on a cane & warns the crossers at the light to mind the sidewalk cracks "for the sake of your dear Old Mother, save her soul," & says it not just once to cue you, but a second time, in a minor key, *for the sake of your dear Old Mother,* & then a third, to cinch the hex like a girth just here, under your ribs, the way a dancetune sweetens & deepens & rides you with every refrain, & despite yourself you watch your hooves, you change your gait, you pick a wayward way around the cracks, obeying superstition not your own, but hers, the mother melody's, maybe, the triple chord you swapped your soul for at the crossroads, primitive, trivial blues, a blues of you & of me & of the hunchbacked figure their meeting makes, with a one & a two & a onetwothree, outriding, outriddling your staid & spent & solitary earthbound self & mine.

Black Swan Pas de Deux

Both yes & no,
  I play me & you
play you. A little
  dance-duet. Strange:
wherever you move
  the sound is broken
glass—where I follow
  it's the running
of blood. To someone
  else I'd say, Keep that
heart shut! Don't lend that
  song a body! No
chance of staging whole-
  ness without a
whole house of gore
  to answer it.

To you I say, Hold
  me close. &
spin. & hold
  me close. & spin.
Muscle tissue's
  messy—no one taught it
to squeeze on blades,
  shards, splinters, or keep
going when not hooked up.
  But look! How they
fit right in
  they fit right in.

Triptych in Pieces

A chord's, let's say, one dosado
on three imperfect pitches, do-mi-sol,
matched to miss & marry so.

A pitch, let's say, 's one frequent sound
ahum in the three dimensions, up & down
& straight ahead in circling round.

& let's say time's one tempo poured
out on the piecemeal immaculate parquet floor
of *was* & *is* & *will be* in accord.

Rondo alla Turca

In the backmost molar, a sandgrain lies in a cleft & hides. Irreducible, my atomy, you will not root or rot, you will not disintegrate. Things used to appear complete with a place to put them—bread to box, coin to cup, dish to drain. The skull was a good jug—hands, its stand—lungs, brown bags drawn tight at the throat—heart, aluminum kick-the-can, home-free heart—what number of vessels, & vessels for vessels, one in another, orbits in order, the sieve in the mixing bowl in the soup tureen—brush, rinse, spit, brush, rinse, what is clogged, jar loose, what is loose, sift through, what is sifted, store—mountains smooth to the tune of that file, to drill & dynamite yield up their scree, their terracotta shards, their metals, prized & unprized—once in a while, the unclassified stone, unknown, & rougher than rasp of instruments—listen, here in the teeth, you are mine, the odd-sided die I can do nothing with. Let's shoot craps, just us two, & if I win, you will be changed into something rounder than rain, round as the dryspeck bound at the core of the drop. & if I win? comes the echo. If you win, go on grinding away, till my mouth is a hole in the ground.

Museum Piece

Funereal amphora, two scenes intact:
Obverse: in fine red-figure, an orator
Midstride beside the sea, reciting Homer.
For practice, mouth swollen with stones—click-clack
Of their eloquence, grate of Oceanic
Surf against shingle in inarticulate meter.
He is young, he is absolute! He wants the ear
Of the deaf sea, the deaf dead in the scene he chants:
Reverse: Achilles & Patroclus, seated.
They play at dice carved from a Trojan's teeth,
& roll them into his helmet, upturned for a dish,
& wager the coin they took from under his tongue.
Hermes, patron of gamblers, patron of thieves,
& guide in that mine of souls toward which, headlong,
They hurtle, looks on, unseen, white-figured in ash.

Dicer

Canary of mine, of the mine of the mind,
Bright pip in cathedrals of salt,
Each jackhammer stroke
Outsings you, each echo
Cusses more grains from the vault
Than your beaknotes kiss
In their lifetime underground.
The salt collects in symmetrical forms, like dunes
In an hourglass,
But vast—so the diesel tractors gnawing their base
Seem sandbox toys, the miners, ants
With ants' intentions,
Helmet lamps
Throwing out faint alleys of light that never close.
Death's maw, great gourd, is spare & immaculate
As this sparkling room,
Both still & deep,
Stirred by the hiss & fade of funneled salt.
Who listens to you tasting it, testing it?—
Your trills that keep trembling down without a falter,
Like rainwater drained from the eaves into a drum.
—But your silence they *would* hear,
Something wrong with the air,
Stop everything,
& rush to the rickety lift to be hoisted up.
What faith in a pair
Of teaspoon lungs,
To stake one's all on their continuing!
Noise machine, yellow wind-up gaud,
Here you are most absurd

& mean the most.
Is it the idea of other worlds
Or the stone & the salt you were born to
You're always praising? Or cursing? It must
Be the gall in your beak you've sworn
To best, to outlast,
Your dicer's need to spill what you hold.

ANIMATO

A body of water. Curvature in the millrace. A river with limbs of a child! hairless, jointless, kicking at air. Why this is a form. Why this is *the* form. Because—no, not by cause—by origin. *Slow down,* say the banks, but the river's ear shuts quick as it opens, becomes a hamstring or a pumping arm. It speaks in current & diverging. The banks lean back to keep their balance, or get washed away. Why this is a form. Why this is *the* form. By cause? By origin, as water down the smoothest grade will snake & turn for sinuous is the form of flowing. Why this is the form—no cause, no cause but origin—a higher place, a lower place, a hide-&-seek with crevices & ever downward rooms, slipping, scenting ever seaward, now dammed, now driven, but in its falling shifting gouging running it counter saying no & laughing no & turning no & again no & for an instant filling all relations from shore to shore in shape of one smooth beast that comes to the mill & came to the mill & spoke & speak & say how you came to the mill & felt the spoked flywheel flutter inside you & found & feigned & find a whole new life.

Old Motion Picture

What heaves against the wooden slats
Of the millwheel down at your summer place
Is fluid & wholly animal. It sweats,
Machinery keeps spinning, grist
Sifts in the lungs of the father's children.
Below the house, their games of cops-
&-robbers carry them screeching down
The hill, feet caught in the speed of the slope.
The afternoons run on & on
This way, till it's no longer clear
Who is after whom. They grow
Out of their loose clothes by the hour,
& play their swimming game in the millpond,
Marco Polo, or *Where am I now?*

After Proteus

Come walk with me beside the millwheel turning
& speak to me as if you're speaking to
the river, too. The names for everything,

however short or shy of what you're thinking,
what you're meaning, still can, still *do*
come. Walk with me beside the millwheel, turning

though now the mill's been out of use so long
no one remembers it, a place you stare right through
the river to the names for. Everything

possible rose & fell on the single tongue
that drove the shaft that drove the stone anew.
Come, walk with me. Beside the millwheel, turning

from one word to another, from one person
to another, *you* will start becoming *you,*
the river. To the names for everything,

for this side-by-side, this more-than-fellow feeling,
we lend our measure: one-two, one & two.
Come walk with me beside the millwheel turning
the river to the names for every thing.

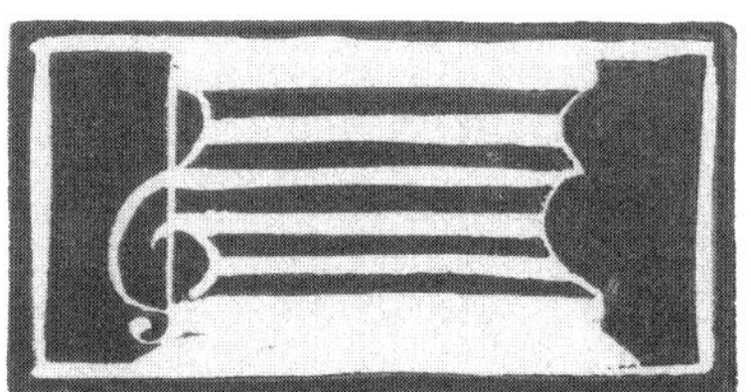

Field Guide

He simply happens by, of **Homo Animalis** *neither the first nor last but with a round Eye toward both, & lacking, therefore, the Stereoscopic Vision needed to walk a straight Line up a Hill. Feet, for that Matter, are none too versatile, One given to Blisters & the Other prickly with poor Circulation, in need of frequent Stomps. A Roughness in Words, perhaps a Contempt for them, marks his Evolution, but he listens well, & remembers Things. He talks to Himself, or to the Air, whom he calls* **Mother,** *& sometimes She replies, though what he knows of Love is lonely, lonely, lonely.*

~

Born of a straightedge & a grafted braid
I come loping, limping, humble, hungry, looking
For origin & answer. My pied tongue licking
Bootsole, shoeblack, long since hybridized.

Dumpster-eyed, one of the half-breed scavenger brood
With fingered wings & no call, flocking
To a dying animal, I on Pelican
Earth arrive to find, expiring, breeze:

& the wind said:

Snail-eyed, you tenderer
of speech, than speech,
these are vestal fingertips that search
your pelt, not flies or
leeches to twitch
to, under, at, off, for.

Habitat is varied & various Scrub Country. Often seen foraging for food along Cuttings, Edges, Scree Slopes, Margins, Verges, Cusps, Seams, Rims. Courtship Rituals unknown. Behavioral Data inconclusive. Nomadic. Hide tends to Infection & so covered. Juvenile Plumage unknown. Structure of Eye unknown. Tool-Use widely documented. Also able with Signs, though far from systematic; some Signs (audible, visible) assumed to signal Nothing At All. Active by Day & by Night. Whereupon vast Majority of other native Species wary, less vocal. Combs Beaches deliberately. Omnivore. Known to consume Carrion. Sometimes consumes Nothing At All for long Stretches. Infrequently, drinks.

~

Eat relics, eat offal, or pare the dinner down
To bitter bone, sweet marrow. Flesh is for
Altars, winters, fatting pigs for fair.
Stitch my side with breath at its sharpest drawn.

She made, she molded me. Once, from deep in the dunes
She drew the clavicle, sand-smooth, of a friar
Who'd had his hermitage there some years before.
Unbarrelled, umbilical stave—my dry quill drained:

& the wind said:

I licked you to a point
as a bear her young.
Of his renunciation & my tongue
you come, my skeletal boy,
to be, a nothing hooped into lung,
bone-needle threaded with a hollow flight.

For he transforms. For his whole Person is both tragic & comedic Mask. A Mask being like a Word he wears. For he has Words in exchange for Things. & he, without a Stitch of Clothing on, is shaggy with Words as if in Fact he were a Beast. For each As If is no less than a Self-induced biochemical Mutation by which he shifts his Shape, Mood, Manner, & yet stays whole. For he is cracked & crazed with Wholeness. For the Dream of Wholeness is one & the one sacred Mark of a Human Beast. For by this Mark did his Skullplates treble in Capacity. For he is the more Human the more multiple his Mind. That Mind descended, via a natural Selection, from all the noble ancient Lineage of **Being**. *But only in part. For* **Not Being** *was equally his noble ancient Mother. For even out of Wedlock she was passing fair, this sudden Apparition in his very Midst, in the Midst of Beasts, of Misery, surfacing out of the Ocean, sweeping through the Sacred Grove, grafting & grooving into his Person, his Solarplexus, a little Gasp, a Nest, a little breeding Emptiness, a Brothel hollowed out for this Vibrato:* **Nothing**—*by Her was he, in Part, conceived.*

~

A cipher does not suffer, not from use
Or disuse, not from being bled to symbol
(O rose of no garden) or stripped down past the simple
(This stigma, this style) to namelessness.

Whisper my watchword in the solemnest
Hall, in the banquet room, the unsiegeable castle,
Cold keep of our cryptic treasures: this tremor: a bat
Holed up in the battlements slips off his rest:

& the wind said:

Some night when air's a veil, & the old sextant
loses what stray star signaled there a moment,
think of the thoughtless animal that man
used to have been
for whom this nothing was native element
and will be once again.

Aged nine Months & upwards, Inition of dominant Trait. (Precedes always full Function of Hands & Feet.) Id est, mouths Objects at Random. Ea sunt, round Stones, hollow Cups, worn Coins, Snail Shells. Gums toothless, aiding in this primitive Stage of Sensation. Objects thrust into Jaw Cavity, rolled round, screened, scanned, catalogued, spat out or swallowed. Percentage of the latter, vomited. Shape of Object thereupon available to Recall, & voiced in Reverse from Bowels, Larynx, Uvula, exempli gratia: "Cup," "Coin," "Stone," "Shell." Jaw doubly hinged to increase Capacity. Ingests Fragments of Landscape: Cliffface, Sluiceway, Sundog, Fata Morgana. After Accession of Teeth, Marks inscribed upon said Objects. Mouthprint incised on Soap or Spoon. Pips on Gambling Dice. Gashes in True Gold, spotless the Counterfeit.

~

Fossiliform, my own beaked face impressed,
Caesarean graffito in the rock.
I listen for archaic thundercrack,
Echoic, clue from a marly mantle prized.

For what I love I double, doubting not
My own commandments, graving images.
I feed the chert that steads me; what famishes
I render to God, my glyph, my syllable ingot:

& the wind said:

Thou shalt not serve
the food once tasted.
Thou shalt not revive
a shape exhausted.
& never shall savor come to waste
on lips that say the thing they save.

Coming-of-Age Ritual takes place alone, & without Instruction. Incident attested in oldest Annals. Dressed in Hides, exits known Terrain, emptyhanded but for a Staff of White Pine, fresh-cut & resinous. Pilgrims three Days, no Stopping. Drawn, perhaps by migratorial Impulse, to Headland jutting north & seaward. Actions hereupon, bizarre & unaccountable. Lean-to constructed at Cliff-Edge, with single Door opening over Abyss. Thereafter, Subject disappears. Lean-to Searches turn up Nothing At All. A Leap presumed. Leap has never yet been witnessed. Staff, perhaps, buoys sinkable Body through Waves. That Word Perhaps denotes an Inference. Known Subjects sometimes re-identified Years afterward, occupying Territory in Antipodal Hemisphere. Fate of unknown Subjects remains unknown.

~

Kid, in goatskin—time gone fat as a snail's pace,
Sliming down sunny hours—I lowered despair
Out onto that disappointed bridge, King's Pier,
Becoming, at the edge, its longest-lost piece,

A curio of interstellar space—
One pretty thing that is at last—past prayer,
Past void or stardom—held hard to heart, use-poor
& purposeless, but whole beyond suppose:

  & the wind said:

      First you, then I—
      So father, daughter,
      all God's spies,
      hold the door
      for one another:
      curtsy & fly.

Tide out, Sun up, the Choughs are catching the first Updrafts off Cliffs, black Laundry thrown to the Pole, or winging the Midway, or folded in Stoop. Chee-ow, Chee-ow, is the Cry. Crosslegged in Seawrack & Boulders, moaning sore Feet, he hunches. A Ring of rough red Marbles, twenty or thirty, cordons him off. In rhythmic Time to the Waves, with high-held Stone Pestle he bashes each with Method, one after one, into Powder. This collecting in a sort of rude Clay Jar, this Jar he brings down to Seas-Edge, to which some Additives of purple Shells & Salt. Mixes. A Shout. With a scabbed Forefinger he paints Face, he reds Clothes, he runs naked between Rocks, Chee-ow & again Chee-ow, he tips whole Jar back & drinks. Drops hard down in Stupor, Mouth wide, & will not stir until Tomorrow.

~

Doctoring stones takes hands, no chisel, no blade.
Pressure-tuned & -tendoned, palms & calluses
Calibrate as fine as a set of scales.
Deal gently. Pound & be kind. One slab will yield

Her cursive, hieroglyph, vein of magmatic blood:
Grind this grain. Harvest this dust. Alchemical
Sparks & water make dye of Protean coals,
Your rock-raw motherload, to spell out bold:

& the wind said:

What new clothes! Red ones!
Laid out fresh-dyed on the bleaching stones,
all variations on the body's themes,
how you minister to them,
their creases, bending to them like patients.

I love you, I will fray each one at every seam.

That Subject is subject to our Watch, he knows. That Subject detects at once the Lighting of Eyes upon him is assured beyond Question. For if observed, he straightway changes Course or Custom or Habit or Mask till unobserved again. Nor thereafter resumes a Natural Direction, but once forced to vary, does not cease from Variation. & therefore must his Motions be inferred from Prints & Echoes & how the Sparrow skitters off the Path in the Field before him.

~

Marionetted in seines of tic & urge,
Mesh of muscle, mess of nervework hemmed
In with sensation stitches, thrills & harm
Dovetailing to the tune of doors ajar:

Attune: there's lightshaft on the parquet floor:
& like the catch of caught sight clicking home
Or quick unlidding of some Pentelic herm
Disfigured, it dismantles my disfigure:

& the wind said:

Handsome! Don't let some wince of light
unmake or -man you. Look
for me in flags & kite-
tails, heads of black-
eyed susans leaning all one way. But let
them look at you & do you look straight back.

Manifests Interest in own History. Instance: watches Shadow walk in Step. Gaze therefore acts as Sundial, though no Evidence that Use is made as such. At rest, Contrapposto Alignment of Parts preferred, Torso aimed ahead, Face behind. This Pose perhaps triggered by Angle of Sunlight (crepuscular, autumnal), though Hypothesis untested. Known to follow Footprints for Miles, others' & own, across Mud, Silt, Scree, Sand, Leaflitter, & Granite (when wet). Tracks slowly. Synchronized with Prey but rarely. Follows forward & backward & both, till All Prints indecipherable. Once Path becomes established, veers & begins Anew.

~

As sweet is lined by scent, so trace the light
By where it's not, the nest-knot at the heart
Of green the June forsythias inherit,
Brood out of reach & sight, dark distillate.

Up field, down streambed, over glacial shale
Tilled fine enough to register & keep
A hatchling's step, I turn, & I escape,
My dumb beak pipping at this single shell:

& the wind said:

Icier trails
once ran this way.
Meltwater fills
the weighted womb,
& what you are, & what I am,
is parsed out piecemeal in articulate hills.

One of few Species known to perform Selfsame Burial, alone, & with no Assurance of Re-emergence. Perhaps without Expectation. Without Desire, perhaps. No Stone to mark Place, no Music to mark Time. Music as such. Wind an irregular Toll, Pitch variable, Timbre variable, according to Shape & Coil & Conch of given Ear. Grasslands of sandy Soil often chosen Terrain for said Operation. Hole dug, haltingly, & somewhat broader than Body Width, less deep than Depth. Long enough, however. Once completed, Digging Stick cracked & discarded. Entombment begins with ritualized Fall, once, twice, or in Series. Stands at Foot, places Pebble or Shell under Tongue, drops backward, as in Snow. Repeats. Repeats till motionless. Piled Earth silts down to smooth the Grave, but never fast enough. Exploring, you will find Hummocks, Years apart.

~

Consigned to no one time, but to continuous
Tempos, their racings, my racings, their easing, mine.
Epitaph: *What have I been? A servingman*
To pulse, its wax-&-wane, & in between a

Stamp of halfblooded nature, uninked, innocent,
That took & gave impress, that could command
No atmosphere its own, but a common moon
Hitting horizon, as cratered as mountainous:

& the wind said:

Of what are you ashamed?
You never gave
consent to this, to be set down alive,
to be made hush & tame.
I pass your tomb
but by your leave.

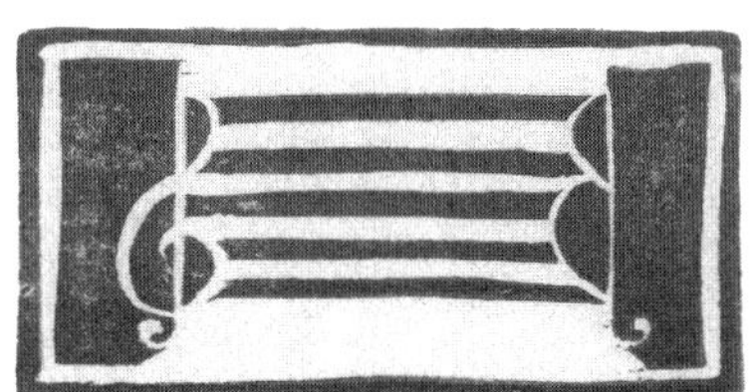

Adagio Quasi Immobile

I dreamt I was with St. Francis, circled by birds. They were shy, expectant: maybe Orpheus had ushered them down from the air in the air's language, but from this man came only odd little hiccoughs & hums & whistles, emitted by chance, like the ticks of a wound-down clock. He held out thistle seed that slipped through his fingers & could be had by darting in behind him as he walked. He made an awkward human & an awkwarder bird, stooped & gangly, thick of beard, thin of face. "Francis," I said, "you've done your part, they've eaten. We'll be late for prayers." He was easing his hand out to a blushing finch, which hopped away. "How long might it take," he asked, "for birds to think of me as one of their saints?"

Now the One, Now the Other

No doubt I too will fall under the prediction
& someday soon will say, "That little time
I spent with birds," in the vague unforgivable way

An elder speaks of an old self in his bed.
& no doubt now, defensive, I should say, "Elder,
I have slept with a hawk on my hand, & bled

Where her talons hit, & still fed her flesh from it,
& watched her eyes watching for movement in the grass,
& saw the grass move there." & true enough,

There is something of birds in me, & true enough,
My eyes will never be yellow & hard as the hawk's.
Do you mark how life gets filled, the crevices

Between—now the one, now the other—where some spirit hides,
Where that hunted thing prays not to be heard?

After Rimbaud

It's been found!
—What? —Eternity.
It's the sea overrun
  With sun.

My soul's eternal.
Run on entire
Through the night alone
& the day on fire.

That's how you're loose
From common prayer,
From human hymn.
Your wing is strung . . .

Not to hope. Erase.
Erase *In the beginning*.
Just knowing, just being,
Is plenty high on the cross.

Erase tomorrow.
Pieces of silk over fire.
  What burns in you
  Is the one vow.

It's been found!
—What? —Eternity.
It's the sea overrun
  With sun.

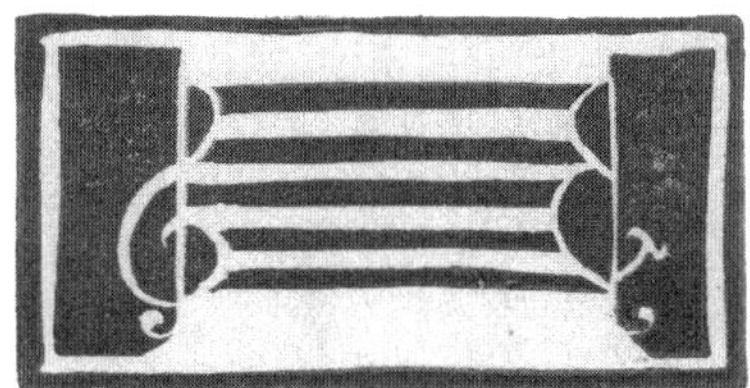

Scherzo

I dreamt I was with St. Francis among the birds. He had not called them, as others have said. He had been doctoring stones. The sea glinted & mocked. He took gravel in hand, rubbed each piece with a thumb, licked it, held it between his teeth, replaced it. This was the work of a madman, & I told him so. & he answered me, saying, "& if I do not minister to the pebble, which my feet grind to dust, which has naught but its own weight for pay & its face for love, how then shall I minister unto myself, whose maladies are in the inarticulate air & my distances from birds?" I swore, & called him lunatic, & it was then I beheld the starlings, long tight scarves of them swirling, folding, re-infolding up & down the beach upon themselves, a tidal wave come loose from its moorings. When they came overhead, like the secret mechanism of *Aurora Borealis,* they seemed suddenly to feel their own weight & drift to earth, & there being not a tree in sight settled to roost on Francis & on me as on two sawhorse scarecrows, in our hair, on our arms, in our rags. So thick were they on the road, it seemed paved with a shifting flint & mica. The racket of wings & voices set my scalp afire, & Francis was bending down for another stone.

Lookout

You think of those Roman soldiers standing guard
Somewhere at the edge of their language, a sentry-post
With commanding views of the valley north and west
Out past the nearest hills, horizonward.

No longer colonizing with the sword,
A lighter touch now, running the eyes across
Toothed ridges, muffled in the manifold blues of distance,
Named in the tangled tongues of uncivilized hordes.

And then, September, hawks lift off from those hills,
All aimed in one direction, passing through
Without password, without permission, their fanned tails
Flying colors you've never paid attention to
Till now, beautiful, barbarian syllables,
A whole sky, unopposed, invading you.

From the Inside Out

How the player-piano plays itself,
 or how the thunderhead mounts in silence,
  how a locomotive wails on its trestle,
   full of precarious balance,
    from the inside out.

How frost heaves, or sap runs,
 how a bloom or berry plumps to a whole,
  how meltwater spreads in the old millpond
   come April (though it takes a while)
    from the inside out.

Anachronisms, every one!
 Things I was told before I'd learnt
  to see for myself—the mill long gone
   before it meant what it meant
    from the inside out.

Only late October keeps turning its wheel,
 too cumulus-high to find in a book:
  red leaves, last leaves, churned up wild
   as notes under nobody's hands, & look,
    from the inside out,

the minutes still blooming into hawks,
 sluicing down the horizon-ties
  on steel-smooth, north-south tracks,
   & then, for the first time, your eyes
    from the inside out

spread themselves in concentric rings
 —as if the temperate vision were
  itself a migratory thing
   & felt the cold press of winter
    from the inside out—

or, scaling the wind a second, pause
 as the red-tail does when up it swings
  into a kite, & piano keys
   are rippling down the length of its wings
    from the inside out.

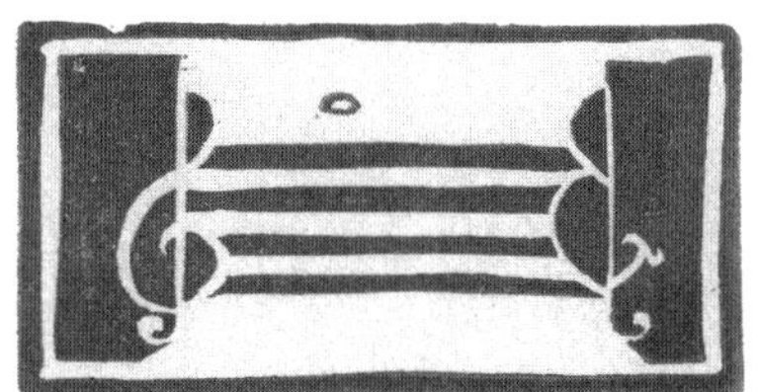

DANZA MACABRA

I dreamt I was with the birds, too many to name, too many to feed, & some were already preying on one another, pinning them down, jays eating wren-chicks, hawks eating jays, pluming them feather by feather to get to the breast-meat, slowly, thoroughly, the victims neither killed nor kept alive, but simply enduring until they died, sometimes before their eyes were gored, for eyes are the beak's one access to the skull, or else before the gizzard was nicked out & set aside, exact as surgery, for gizzards are full of grit, & entrails waste, though the livers could not be left, for the liver is rich & dark—but sometimes not, they lasted longer, their eyes stayed open, blinking, till they were out, & their beaks stayed open, not screeching or wailing, simply open, till their hearts were out, or after, & sometimes the hawk would stop working the breast & shift to the wings & begin plucking there, feather by feather, no more ferocious than the chickadee that shells your sunflower seed, & this was happening everywhere around me, the ground was gizzards & entrails & beds of stray feathers plumped by the wind like blown snow, & I for once knew just what to do, there was nothing to do, I shut my eyes & sang my same old simple song in all directions. You keep on seeing, only louder.

After Montale

Bring me a sunflower to transplant
In this soil of mine burnt dry with salt,
& all day long I'll show the reflecting blues
Of heaven the old distress of its yellow face.

What's dark tends toward illumination;
Bodies sap themselves into a flux
Of colorings: as in music. Vanishing
Is, finally, the fortune of fortunes, luck of lucks.

Bring me the stalk that leads one straight
To where there rise these fair-haired transparences,
Where life wears out to essences;
Bring me the sunflower gone insane with light.

Hymn to Hermes

From the pub door
the spill of voices,
pebble-slide & -slur
when listened to together,
their cross purposes

closing, as runoff rain
from separate channels
evacuates a mountain
in one stream. World-hum. Plain-
note, descended from: Box turtle,

stethoscope to the thaw/flow-
frost/heave rivermud,
heard that vectoring *go*
of the geese as if Apollo,
who moves always from a

distance, had left the earth.
She digs with her slow spades.
Ribs heaving. Shell-making. Above her
the banks freezing, seizing tighter
than cramped muscle. Pulse like the dead's,

fór the dead's. Eight minutes.
Beat. Eight minutes. Beat.
Count out the long units
of emergence, blood-music in its
infancy, you who wíll be

taking her up in the springlands
& laying her back on a stone
with two immortal hands
to hallow, hollow out &
stretch with gut, your bone-

instrument. In the past,
desiring sound but needing
a need, an emptiness
to verb over, a glass
to make & lose one's living

in, I thought sacrifice
took killing one's own mind
& setting it down on some high
seat or other, saying, "Christ,
son of Abraham, I am in

thy service, pluck out my heart."
I say, God, any god,
make me a lyre of tur-
tle shell, make me a lyre
to sing into, black sod

to spring through, make river-veins
still moving under still-
unbroken ice, make skin
so sound it sounds & strains
& dies against its will.

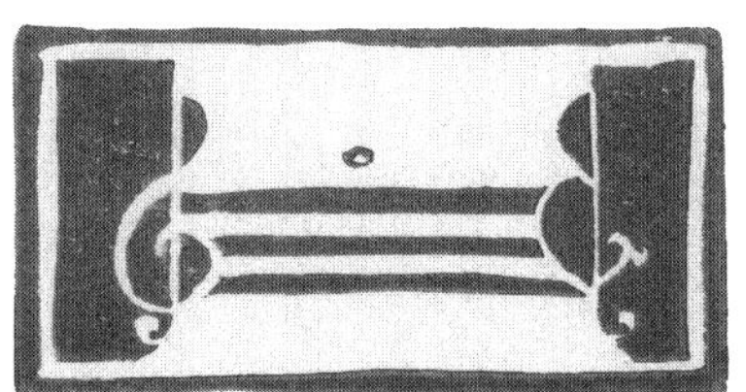

Poco a Poco Crescendo

Sweet Regress! Remember the dance we called the Sweet Regress? Remember the man from the city who showed us the steps? Village girls, crowd round! & we crowded round by the fountain & he showed us the steps. By then it was last week's dance in the city, but blind as we were, we didn't know or care—how long has it been since I thought of the Sweet Regress? His feet went a mile a minute, or they go like mad in the memory of it—the figure they made slapping the stones! You better step to the right, kickstep to the left, & shuffle-back-shuffle on back, way back, shuffle&ashuffle way back. A washed-up newspaperman, can you believe it, but he could've been Fred Astaire for all we knew or cared, & we ran home to show our mothers the Sweet Regress. At dinner my legs went on miming it out like mad in the air, & after the table got cleared, she & Papa danced whatever dance they danced—they had dancing class after school, can you believe it—& I stepped to the right & I kicked to the left & shuffle&ashuffle on back, way back—our black&white collie barking like mad, & rounding us, hemming us in, like back in his sheepdog days as he probably was for all he knew or cared, he was howling & hemming us in, can you believe it, as blind as he was, we stepped to the right & kicked to the left & the whole next week the talk was the man from the city & the Sweet Regress.

After Troy

& you know—have you known?—how this one goes—
Cassandra—in her city & then in another—
As first in her memory & then in the slow
Siege of its happening—went down together
With the press of people, whooping, incredulous,
To see the horse on the shore, the city fathers
High as the tide, & already the centerstage boys,
Adrenaline-wired, laying the rollers beneath her—

& the gates like feet that have forgotten the steps
Flare slowly open, remembrance has this sound,
Wall-pigeons startle, & washerwomen snap
Black laundry like flags—*it's Agamemnon returned*
From the wars—as out at the ebbing sea-rim weeps
A prophetess eating ashes, ashes & sand.

Medieval Memory Palace

Mt. Auburn Cemetery

Gardens within gardens: lichened stone
Rayed out in boxwood hedges, fuchsia plots,

Pansies in polygonal raised beds,
A central fountain, paths, another fountain.

What place is walled or islanded enough
To house the bodiless, dedicate due room?

You spent & formal pilgrim, newly come,
Lay down your irises, arms of rhododendron,

(Or if not these, then something a little like)
Within wrought-iron solemnized & soundless—

Soundless but for fountains, & wind in the leaves, a sound
Of wide orchestral static, spun round a source.

Frame after frame, world involving world,
The whole ahum with old geometry:

Boys race bikes down intersecting paths,
No less in sympathy with circumstance

Than the potter swelling the urn upon her wheel,
Who fashions her antique mood in the whirr of a treadle;

Or as orioles in streamside willows weave
Of scavenged flower-ribbons & colored string

(Not these, but something a little like, a little near)
The more than masterful jugs for wombing her,

Invisible, within the greenest crepe,
On high, above the currents, here, that sweep

Forever toward utmost periphery
& midmost rest, forever toward.

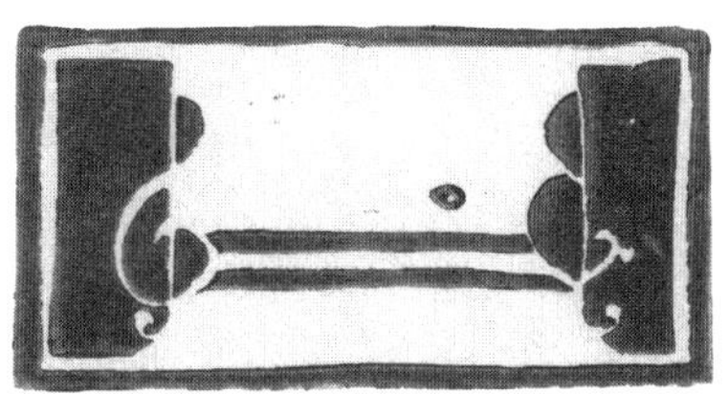

Tempo Mortale

Those blind-born, lovelorn, lonesome-sad-&-mournful men,
  all dead, keep waking up this morning being been
mistreated, mama, in the worst of low-down ways,
  with worried minds, same clothes as yesterday's,
a midnight outbound train the one sound answer to
  most anything—they sing in my living room,
bedroom, barroom, boxcar, corncrib, dance hall, or falling
  asleep in their boots, or none, or one, or in ball-&-
chain of convict or ghost they can't shake, get quit of, leave
  behind for good, no more than the woman you love,
the place you was raised, the things you seen, the reasons you had
  this morning for feeling like dying the way you did.
How happy you'd have to be to be so awful sad
  in just three chords, the one to say you cried
for days & days, the second to cry a second time,
  the third to quit your crying in a rhyme
that promises you'll end your good-for-nothing ways.
  So long as the singer has something to praise,
—God, Achilles, the moon,—I used to think, he has it all.
  He ain't got it all. Blind Willie McTell,
going up the country with your Statesboro Blues,
  let me put on your light, light traveling shoes.

Blues for Papa

Siren says what most you happen to hear,
Being for most the forms that being takes
& treasures: childhood's bird, its blare, tokens
Like handsels, Hansel-stones, the sawhorse chair
That wears your weight, that gallops four feet through years
Of earth, this place, & its musical lunatic
Swoon of a homing sense that says *all yours*,
& makes you name your son Telemachus.

& for most, that's what she sang. Only for you
Who stood apart, at the prow, an empty air
Blew emptier, as a head or hollow hums
Around some one idea, sécreting hymn,
& the wind did what you would have it do,
Nothing, & feeling this, we rowed the faster.

Milkman

Not till this old-fashioned morning, Son House singing
through fifty pushups, fifty situps, some pain-
ful stretches into lower registers

that can't be reached, on a skipping record,
Got a letter this morn—, Got a letter this morn—,
not till I rifled every kitchen cupboard

& poked through sacks of nothing but dry goods,
& the fridge the same, no eggs, no meat, no greens,
& I, who have never been poor, sat down, tired,

not till then did I think about the milkman,
a real man to my parents' generation
but myth to mine, who'd come in the dawn & leave

two bottles on the stoop beside the door,
uncapped, they said, & frothy, &, sometimes, warm,
narrow-necked bottles that flared out like the bell

of a gramophone, like the mouths of changeling twins
you found each morning, unswaddled, unexplained,
& take in full, & put out empty, & think

no more about than mail arriving twice,
or papers by evening, or kids after school, or sun
going up & down by everybody's watch.

But now your bottle floats up into mind,
milkman, minstrel, waylaid messenger,
without a message, without milk, without

even a sun to slip slow through your glass,
& you say, *Hush—I thought I heard her call*
my name, & suddenly your being gone

delivers me a second time into the world,
brimful, & fuller, maybe, than before,
having had no taste of what there'd be to lack.

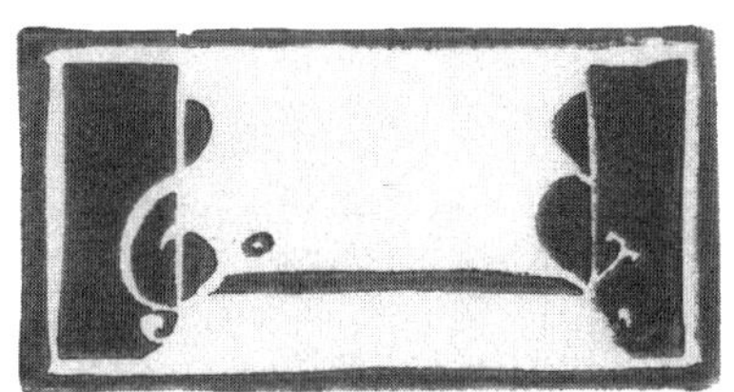

Minuetto

I levitated just the once or no, call it a leavening in the air's direction, heel to toe, or cancel that & call it a slow sink of the strata on all sides, like keeping your wits about you while it rains, or cancel that, in downpour, down comes the torrent & there you be, buoyant as striders on a rising pool, the view's improving, cancel that, it's grand, it's magisterial, the surface packed & porous & draining where it brims but you with your wits about you, riding the suds of the minute, mariner-like, or cancel that, like a bloom of the waterlily letting out line, taproot & tether, or cancel that, no cord, your wits about you drowned, & you unmoored, tiptoe, no cancel that, you're leavening, abrim on a pool that rises, minute by minute, the minute's your element, or cancel that, your element's to tread your element, or cancel that, to tread it down.

After Aphrodite

Most everything born out the froth of phrases
Gets drowned directly after—the mythical
Divinity excepted, whose cockle-shell
Made even less sense than the tidal forces,
Rip currents, undertows, those surfaces
That kiss & part for heavier syllables.
To the fairest... What floats, floats like an apple.
Borne up, that first soprano voice above voices,
Bobbing with seaweed & seawrack—

High A!

as if

Inside the myth-composing ear, gone deaf
& pressed to the chest of a skeletal piano,
A cold-as-marble stethoscope keyed you
A pitch above consideration, life
Trebled, & trembling with fremitus from below.

Of the Relative Motion of Bodies

& neither maze nor veils to speak me plain

—SONG

Like a snail that's learned to walk on tender horns
She moved against the motion of the train
Relenting step by step as only one can
Against her instinctive will relentlessly thrown.

We turned to watch her, every passenger.
She put one hand on a seat at the back of the car
& dropped her purse, which burst like a jar at pressure,
Scattering coins & lipstick on the floor.

They sifted up the aisle, lapped at our feet
Like incoming tide, & like beachcombers we
Stooped for it, deep-sea treasure, picked it up,
& not to help: we put it in our pockets.

Thieves of occasion, how we loved her strange,
We loved her distant. Not having her, but glad
For a token, a bit of mask, some small change
To settle recollection on. We might have had her,

But who in his right mind would turn & speak
His own incomprehensible words that way? Would you?
Would you throw moonlight all the way back to the moon?
Would you throw back this shell you can't give back?

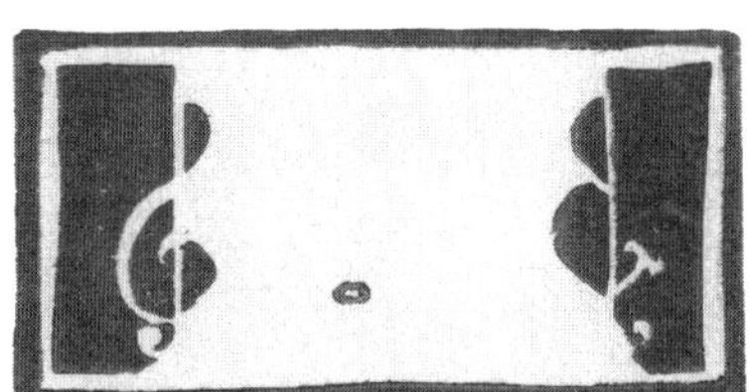

Ballata con Moto

Sing me a little something before bed, & something sweet, sweeter than he & sweeter than she, & make it go on awhile, like the birds, & like the one about the birds, the one who couldn't sing & the other one that could, so they flew around together, in the shadows of the woods, or like the one about the sinner & the one about a saint & the two came to a fountain & dying of a thirst & the sinner said you'd better drink & the saint drank fit to burst & the sinner said you were thirsty & the saint smiled & said yes & said now you drink sinner & the sinner bent & drank & there was nothing left at all but a few drips in the tank & the saint said we forgot the horses & the sinner shook his head, I gave her all my whiskey, every drop I had, & the saint swore something awful & forced him to a knee & whipped him till he bled & the sinner lay there bleeding & left there for to die & the saint gone off for praying so the saint's horse licks him clean.

Eschatologue

It's every isle is peopled with Calibans.
As many, as earthen as we are, we do speak
Well, we hear stuttering or silence
& can get raging drunk on just its music.
Sometimes we come upon marvels even, & long
To hold, like the old farriers, one whole
Black trembling hoof of the trembling
Beast between our knees, a two-inch nail
Between our lips.
                                        & who will hold the bridle?
& who will give the nod? Where is the ostler
With charms of alfalfa under an arm or an apple
In hands rough as currycombs? Who but the pure-
bred massive nickering girl herself to call
By the sacred, hated name of master?

After Caliban

Woke in a sleeping bag sometime past midnight.
The stars my dial, the moon my clock.
The dream I was ripped from had bad intentions,
Knew where to find me, performed its rite.
I shook & shook
Like a dead leaf in a caterpillar tent,
Or like a monarch
Chancing to come to
In the chrysalis, expecting all his limbs
To be changed, made new,
& finding himself no different than before,
Than when he started, only colder.
Of this, the book
Suggested nothing, made no mention.
What once
Used to be straightahead matters
Of getting down your halfadozen lines
By heart & head,
Of knowing to match the mimic gestures,
& places to be at the particular times,
& where your props would be waiting hid
(The firewood, the hazelnuts, the knife) & how
To rant yourself into significance,
Now
Is turned to a foregoing of all those,
An unlettering of every primer learned,
& the heat you keep is the heat of the last day.
By this time of night, it's gone for good,
The sun on the other side of the earth, the full
& unapproachable moon
On high, & each surface heavy with its dew.

What I dreamt,
Though I would rather keep it gone,
Little by little is flickering back—
Pushing open the sliding stable doors,
& the summer swallow rafters empty,
& the Appaloosa mare on her side in the stall,
& forgelight round her like a readied brand,
& under her not hay
But a seething bed of cinders, asphalt-black
For an instant, till
The rush of air from through the opened doors
Takes all the vision up into inferno.

Give us this day
Is always on my tongue,
& then *Forgive us for.*
My life I neither wish nor wish aside,
But let me see that mare
Go cantering,
Riderless,
From one end of the isle to another,
& I renounce the dreaming world forever,
Or else the bliss
Of waking all at once & once for good.

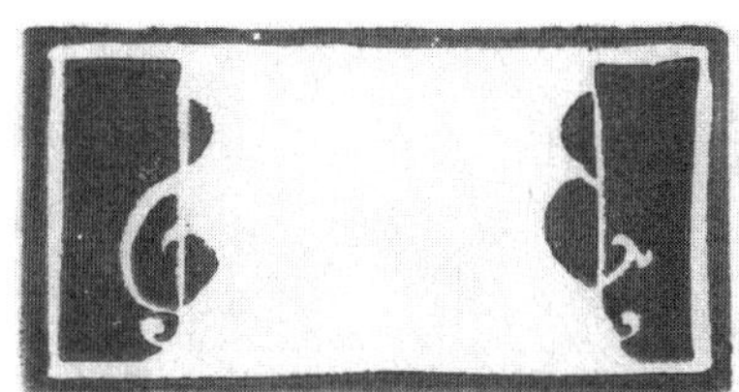

CODA

after Propertius

Travelers say: the shore of the Red Sea
  bristles: miles of bows & bowstrings, miles
of archers, shoulder to shoulder. On each string
  (swear all travelers), an arrow fletched with salt-
breeze, tipped like breakers spangled by light,
  & every quiver full. Or so they say.
That, for a sense of scale. What sea is more
  than a man's own blood? What shafts sharp as desire?
(Or the other way round, perhaps? An idea
  might cipher for the honest-to-goodness thing?
Achilles, Saint Sebastian, all of them?)
  Let loose, let fly at every moment. Feel
in wounds, deep wells; in tidal whelms of pain,
  the holy orders undergone for love.

Loves are the lightest, sing-song poems to sing,
  yet even on the side of Mount Helicon,
birthplace of our own & epic origins,
  you hear their rhythms, not to charm the oaks
from off their roots, or leopards out of wildness,
  but more that a girl should stand stock-still & listen.
That would be fame without end, without frame,
  like watching your own life tower into myth.

I am more than a lover of a beautiful face,
  more than ambitious for her family name.
Not these. But to lie in the arms of a girl who knows
  whereof I spoke, to see her ears glow red
all suddenly, & then to let the silence fall
  around us two, after all words are done.
Good night to the merciless chatter of other people,

the nattering-on about weather, the dying, the dead—
I need no audience save that one embrace.
What I sing, & to whom, are the same.
If I could but reconcile her ear to me,
I'd bear the enmity of all this world
& of another—even heaven's, even God's.

Greenhouse Labyrinth

Sometimes even the truest words go quiet
All the way to silence, & take root there
Like plants that pull their living straight from air,
& hang, of earth still solid part, above it;
Or like *Mimosa,* bashful, touch-me-not,
A clue that hesitates to answer clear
&, in hesitating, makes aware
Of love the fingertips in love with it.

Say the twining heart has what it needs
In way of words. Say it's how it twines.
I walk straight toward you, then turn aside
To another flower. Or say what I mean
Are lips as red as pomegranate seeds
& mute to mine.

PROMISSORY

March's green
is last year's fern,
a few fronds pressed
in winter's book.
What more is there
to say? I still
say love's a sight
in a silent place.
You look & look.
The beaver pond
is steeped in ice.
Maybe decay
heats up the well:
ankle-deep
in rings of melt
stand white-pine snags
where herons build.
If I but knew
your name or where
to meet you, plain
as day I'd press
the lettering
as small in snow
as a red eft's print.

About the Author

HENRY WALTERS was born in Chicago in 1984 and grew up in Indiana and southern Michigan. He studied Latin and Greek at Harvard College, beekeeping in Sicily, and falconry in Ireland. He has worked as a teacher, a naturalist, a practicing falconer, and a steward of a wildlife sanctuary. His poems, translations, and essays have appeared in a range of publications, from *The Old Farmer's Almanac* to *The American Guide to Hawk Migration Studies*, and he is the recipient of *Better Magazine*'s 2013 prize for poetry. He currently lives in the beech and hemlock woods of Dublin, New Hampshire, where he coordinates the New Hampshire Young Birders Club and acts as Secretary for Experimental Living at Dublin School.

THE HOBBLEBUSH GRANITE STATE
POETRY SERIES

HOBBLEBUSH BOOKS publishes several New Hampshire poets each year, poets whose work has already received recognition but deserves to be more widely known. The editors are Sidney Hall Jr. and Rodger Martin. For more information, visit the Hobblebush website: www.hobblebush.com.